D1476909

Terry's aunt, Stella Mae Richardson, holding a family picture with a quilt in the background, similar to the Oscar's Girl Quilt.

QUILTS THROUGH THE CAMERA'S EYE

by Terry Clothier Thompson

Quilts Through the Camera's Eye
By Terry Clothier Thompson

Editor: Kent Richards
Technical Editor: Shannon Richards
Book Design: Cheryl Johnson
Photography: Aaron T. Leimkuehler
Illustration: Lon Eric Craven
Production assistance: Jo Ann Groves

A special thanks to Shiloh Museum of Ozark History in Springdale,
Arkansas and to Marie Demeroukas, Photo Archivist/Librarian, for use
of the vintage photographs.

Published by:
Kansas City Star Books
1729 Grand Blvd.
Kansas City, Missouri, USA 64108

All rights reserved
Copyright ©2007 The Kansas City Star Co.

No part of this book may be reproduced, stored in a
retrieval system, or transmitted in any form or by any
means, electronic, mechanical, photocopying, recording or
otherwise, without the prior consent of the publisher.

First edition, first printing
978-1-933466-40-8
Printed in the United States of America by Walsworth
Publishing Co., Marceline, MO

To order copies, call StarInfo at (816) 234-4636
and say "Books."

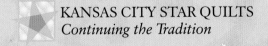

www.PickleDish.com

KANSAS CITY STAR QUILTS
Continuing the Tradition

TERRY CLOTHIER THOMPSON

Terry Clothier Thompson makes her home in Lawrence, Kansas and works in her new studio. There she teaches classes on dating quilts to small groups of women who want to know about the old fabric in quilts, their history and to educate quilt shop owners on how to be an informed seller of historical reproduction fabrics. Terry collects vintage quilts, clothing, quilt tops and blocks to teach her weekend FabriCamp© classes during the late spring, summer and early fall. The classes are taught on Friday, Saturday, and Sunday, but she also schedules a special four-day extended session, that includes a day trip to view other textile collections.

Terry has written three books for the Kansas City Star, "Four Block Quilts," "Libertyville," and "Quilts in Red and Green," co-authored with Nancy Hornback. Look for their sequel "Appliqué for Today from Yesterday's Quilters" in spring of 2008.

Terry also designs reproduction fabrics for Moda. Her impressive collection of vintage fabric c. 1790-1950 inspires her to create authentic looking fabrics for historical based quilts. Look for her new lines of Convenience Cloth in the quilt stores.

For fun, Terry grows flowers to press, then designs small still life pictures using old fabrics, lace and crocheted work. Two children, four grandchildren, and a sixteen-year-old stitch group that meets every week brings her shared friendship and support.

Born into the fifth generation of a Kansas pioneer family, she watched her grandmother and aunt quilt during visits to the family farm called Peace Creek. Her quilting began with the scraps she saved from a dress she made for her daughter, Shannon, in 1967.

Terry has been on the forefront of the current quilt revival. In 1973, she opened The Quilting Bee, a store devoted entirely to quilting—an anomaly at the time. The store was originally at 49th Street and State Line Road and later at Seville Square on the Country Club Plaza. It closed in 1984.

A lover of quilt history, Terry was a principal documentor for the Kansas Quilt Project and a co-author of Kansas Quilts and Quilters, published in 1983 by the University Press of Kansas.

Terry also designs and writes books for Peace Creek Pattern Co., owned and operated by Terry's daughter and her husband Kent Richards. These books are about Terry's pioneering family and the quilts of the 1800-1940's period of America's history. Terry designs marking tools for appliquérs. The "Vine Line"©, and the new "Border Line"© tools may be found in quilt shops or ordered from her web site, **www.terrythompson.com**

"I cannot design a quilt or write a book without including history—women's history and quilt history are interwoven into the history of the United States of America and our Mother countries, England, France, Italy, and Holland."

INTRODUCTION

I collect many quilt and sewing related objects, and one of my favorite collectibles are photographs of people with quilts in the picture. As a quilt historian, these uncommon photos interest me, and when antiquing, I am always thrilled when one shows up in a basket or shoebox of photos in the antique mall. The quilt usually serves as a backdrop behind the people being photographed, laid over a fence, or covering a chair with a baby standing or sitting on the quilt.

While visiting the Shiloh Museum of Ozark History in Springdale, Arkansas, I saw a great photographic exhibit of people and their quilts posing for the camera c. 1890-1930. The museum's rich collection provided the source for five of the photographs that appear in this book, "Quilts Through the Camera's Eye."

Several years after seeing that exhibit, the idea for this book came to me, why not remake the quilts in the photos, with the new reproduction fabrics in the quilt stores of today. In some instances, I simplified the pattern, or changed the set of blocks, and because the photos are black and white, I felt free to "interpret" what colors were used in that time period.

I enjoyed remaking these quilts and want to thank Pam Mayfield, Jean Stanclift, and Karalee Fisher for their superb piecing and appliqué work, and as always Lori Kukuk's remarkable and creative machine quilting. These women's talents make the quilts and my heart sing.

—*Terry Clothier Thompson*

TABLE OF CONTENTS

Oscar's Girl   2

Nellie Stokes' Bow Tie for a Beau   6

Baby Evelyn's Crazy String Quilt   12

Tennessee Waltz   16

"Homemakers Club" Basket   22

County Fair Cotton Candy   30

Annie Roach
Courtesy Shiloh Museum of Ozark History / Lonnie Roach Collection (S-84-19-14)

Quilt top pieced and set by Terry Clothier Thompson
Quilted by Lori Kukuk

OSCAR'S GIRL

QUILT SIZE: 72" x 72"

YARDAGE

*I chose an ecru colored stripe, a black with red dots, a red with black dots, and a large bandana type red print. You want contrast in colors when you piece the squares, so follow **Figure 1** as a guide for placement of squares.*

- 2 1/3 yards of red large print for squares and borders
- 1 yard of light striped shirting for squares
- 2 1/4 yards of black (referred to as black dot in directions) for squares, triangles and border squares
- 3/4 yard of red (referred to as red dot in directions) for squares

DIRECTIONS

Rotary Cutting Instructions: *The cutting directions include a seam allowance. The letter references are for placement there are no templates.*

- Cut 8 - 3" black dot squares. Cut on one diagonal for 16 black corner triangles 'A'. See **Figure 3**.
- Cut 80 – 3 1/2" large red print squares 'B'
- Cut 100 – 3 1/2" white stripe squares 'B'
- Cut 64 – 3 1/2" red dot squares 'B'
- Cut 4 – 3 1/2" black dot squares for the center of blocks
- Cut 20 – 5 1/2" black dot squares. Cut on both diagonals for 80 black setting triangles 'C'. See **Figure 2**.

Sewing Instructions: 4 - 25 1/2" finished blocks

- Follow **Figure 1** for a color chart and **Figure 4** for a piecing guide.
- Lay all squares and triangles out on a table by your sewing machine. Arrange the squares as shown in **Figure 1**. Leave about 1/2" space between rows of squares. This helps you to see the entire row of triangle/squares and triangles.
- Follow the piecing and setting guide in **Figure 4** for sewing each row of squares and triangles.
- Begin by sewing the corner triangle 'A' to square 'B'. Then sew triangle 'C' to both sides of square 'B' this is your first row. Continue sewing the triangle/squares/triangle sequence for each row. DO NOT PRESS ROWS. Return each sewn row to its position on the table. You may press the block after all rows are sewn.
- Sew rows together.
- Repeat for next 3 blocks.

Setting Blocks and Borders: *Measure your blocks and cut borders to fit*

- Cut 12 – 8 1/2" x 26" large red print rectangles for borders
- Cut 9 – 8 1/2" black dot squares for border squares
- Follow **Figure 5** to set border squares and borders.
- Quilt and bind.

BLACK DOT

WHITE STRIPE

RED PRINT

RED DOT

Figure 1

SIDE TRIANGLES

Figure 2

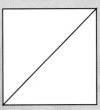

CORNER TRIANGLES

Figure 3

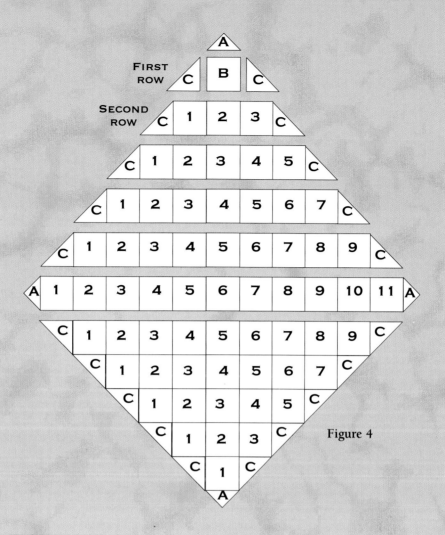

First
Row

Second
Row

Figure 4

Black Dot 8″ x 8″	Red Print 8″ x 25½″	Black Dot 8″ x 8″	Red Print 8″ x 25½″	Black Dot 8″ x 8″
Red Print 8″ x 25½″	3″ Pieced Squares 25½″ Finished	Red Print 8″ x 25½″	3″ Pieced Squares 25½″ Finished	Red Print 8″ x 25½″
Black Dot 8″ x 8″	Red Print 8″ x 25½″	Black Dot 8″ x 8″	Red Print 8″ x 25½″	Black Dot 8″ x 8″
Red Print 8″ x 25½″	3″ Pieced Squares 25½″ Finished	Red Print 8″ x 25½″	3″ Pieced Squares 25½″ Finished	Red Print 8″ x 25½″
Black Dot 8″ x 8″	Red Print 8″ x 25½″	Black Dot 8″ x 8″	Red Print 8″ x 25½″	Black Dot 8″ x 8″

Figure 5

Nellie Stokes and Jackson Eoff
Courtesy Shiloh Museum of Ozark History / Eva Taylor Collection (S-85-51-13)

Quilt pieced by Terry Clothier Thompson and Karalee Fisher
Quilted by Lori Kukuk

NELLIE STOKES' BOW TIE FOR A BEAU

QUILT SIZE: 73 1/2" x 82"

I chose to sew Nellie's Bow Tie blocks into a different set. I think the Streak O' Lightening design works well and makes the quilt more interesting. The fabrics are all dots in bright cheery colors. The lightning streaks and black borders frame and contain the excitement.

YARDAGE

For blocks, setting triangles, and borders
- 1 fat 1/4 each of 4 different dark prints for the bows and knots
- 1 fat 1/4 each of 3 different light prints for bows and knots
- 1 fat 1/4 each of 3 contrasting medium or dark prints for the backgrounds
- 1 fat 1/4 each of 4 contrasting light prints for the backgrounds
- 2 1/4 yards orange print for triangles, corners and binding
- 2 1/4 yards black for borders

DIRECTIONS

Cutting Instructions: *The following cutting dimensions include 1/4" seam allowance.*
- Cut 64 - 3 1/2" light background squares 'A'
- Cut 64 - 3 1/2" dark bow tie squares 'A'
- Cut 54 - 3 1/2" light bow tie squares 'A'
- Cut 54 - 3 1/2" dark background squares 'A'
- Cut 16 - 3" dark squares. Cut the squares on both diagonals for 64 dark bow tie knot triangles 'B'. See **Figure 1**. You will want to coordinate bows and knots so that they will match.
- Cut 14 - 3" light squares. Cut the squares on both diagonals for 54 light bow tie knot triangles 'B'. See **Figure 1**. You will want to coordinate bows and knots so that they will match. (You will have a few extra.)
- Cut 8 - 5 1/8" orange squares. Cut on the diagonal for 16 corner triangles 'C'. See **Figure 2**.
- Cut 26 – 9 3/4" orange squares. Cut on both diagonals for 104 setting triangles 'S'. See **Figure 1**.

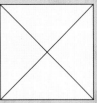

Figure 1

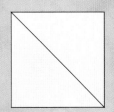

Figure 2

Sewing Instructions:
Light Bow Tie blocks: 27 - 6" finished blocks - 3 rows (rows 2, 4, 6)
- Piece 9 full blocks per row. You will need 7 full blocks and 2 blocks that are cut for each end of the 3 rows of Light Bow Tie blocks. You cannot just cut the blocks in 1/2 as you will lose the 1/4" seam allowance, so you must make the extra blocks to cut following **Figure 4**. Discard the 2nd part of the divided blocks.

Dark Bow Tie blocks: 32 - 6" finished blocks - 4 rows (rows 1, 3, 5 and 7)
- Piece 8 blocks per row.

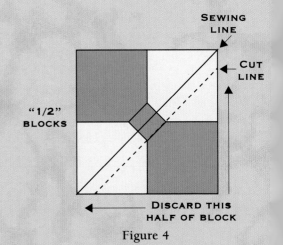

Figure 4

Piecing 1 Bowtie Block:

- Lay out a 4 Patch block from two light and two dark 3 1/2" squares. Do not sew together yet.
- Make a plastic template of the triangle 'B'. Use the template to mark a line with a pencil in one corner of the background squares, on the right side of the fabric. See **Figure 3**. This line serves as a guide. Place the long edge of triangle 'B' (that matches the bow tie fabric) against the pencil line, then sew triangle 'B', right sides together, with a 1/4" seam allowance. Turn triangle over and finger press into corner of the square. It should fit nicely into the corner. Do not cut away the square's corner, as it supports the sewn triangle, which is a good thing.
- Sew the squares into a 6 1/2" Four Patch block. See **Figure 3**.
- Piece 32 dark bow tie blocks and 27 light bow tie blocks.

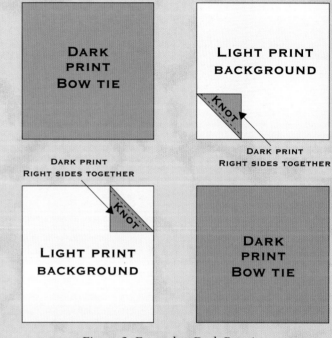

Figure 3: Example - Dark Bowtie

Cutting and Setting Corner Triangles:

- Sew 2 - 'C' triangles to one side of 8 dark bow tie blocks. These will be your top and bottom blocks for the 4 dark rows. Refer to **Figure 5** on the following page.
- All other blocks have a larger side triangle marked 'S'.
- Refer to **Figure 5** and sew triangles 'S' to bow tie blocks then sew blocks together to create rows. There are 4 rows of 8 dark bow tie blocks.
- Sew 'S' triangles to the light bow tie blocks to create 3 rows of 7 add the 1/2 block on the ends of each row. The light bow ties have been set on point. Refer to **Figure 5**.
- Set the rows alternating light and dark. See **Figure 5**.

Borders:

- Cut on the cross grain
- Cut and piece top and bottom borders- 7 1/2" x 60".
- Sew to top and bottom of quilt.
- Cut and piece side borders – 7 1/2" x 82 1/2".
- Sew side borders to quilt.
- Quilt and bind.

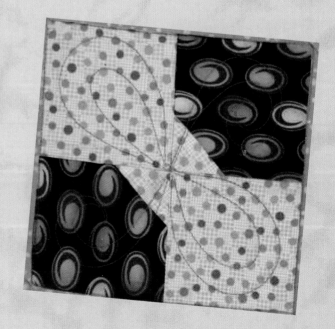

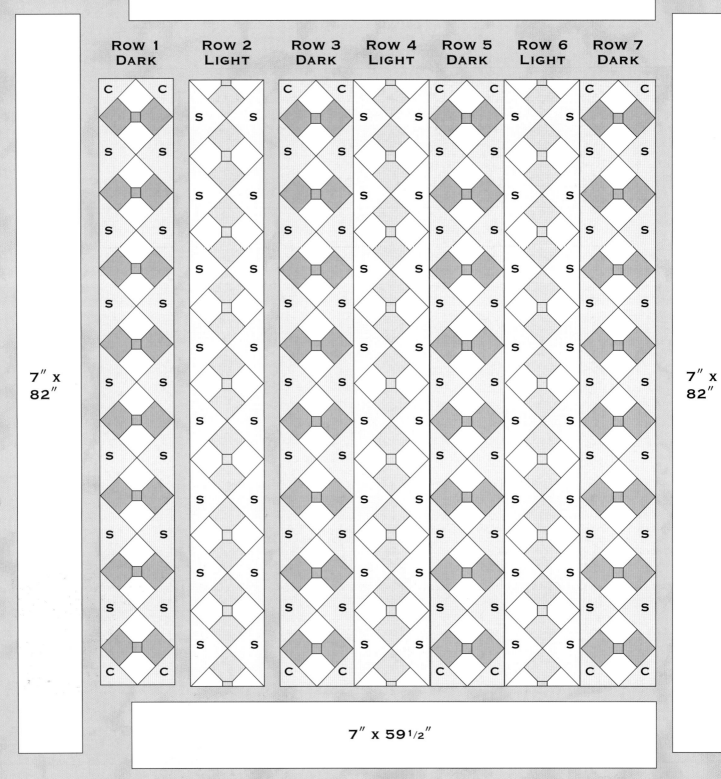

Figure 5

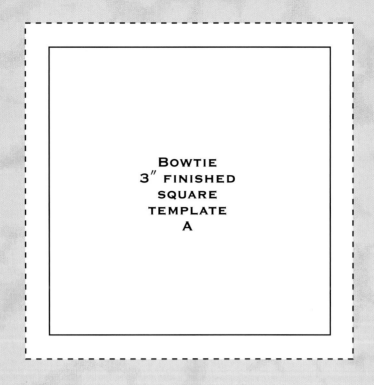

BOWTIE
3″ FINISHED
SQUARE
TEMPLATE
A

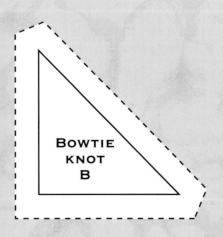

BOWTIE
KNOT
B

TEMPLATES FOR NELLIE STOKES BOWTIE FOR A BEAU

Unnamed baby in picture - Terry named this quilt after her little friend Evelyn Melosa Jones.
Photograph from the collection of Terry Clothier Thompson.

BABY EVELYN'S CRAZY STRING QUILT

Quilt pieced and set by Terry Clothier Thompson
Quilted by Lori Kukuk

BABY EVELYN'S CRAZY STRING QUILT

QUILT SIZE: 63" x 63"

YARDAGE

9 – 20" finished blocks
- 5/8 yard bright pink for 2 - 20 1/2" squares
- 5/8 yard bright purple for 2 – 20 1/2" squares
- 1 1/2 yards of muslin, or scrap fabrics for 20 - 10 1/2" squares of foundation fabric
- 1 1/2 yards black for blocks and quilt borders

Strips: Lengths and widths will vary. Strips will need to be a minimum of 15 1/2" in length. Choose a good variety of bright colors on a black background like the historical reproductions of the neon prints c. 1890-1920 – Terry and Barbara's Moda line, "Ragtime" for example. Throw in some wavy yellow, blue or pink prints. You want a scrappy, jumbled look for the quilt. Use magenta pink, bright greens, brilliant blues, shaded prints, and strips of violet on black.

DIRECTIONS

Cutting Instructions:
- Cut 20 - 10 1/2" x 10 1/2" foundation squares
  Refer to **Figure 1**. The foundation block will be your guide to cutting your strips. Using your rotary cutter (with a new blade) cut strips from your bright fabrics. Cut different lengths and widths, wide and skinny, and at least 2 wedges (wider at one end) for each block to avoid looking symmetrical. The length of the strips decreases in size with the longest for each block needing to be at least 15 1/2". These will be squared up later to your foundation block. We want each block to have it's own wacky lines to create a crazy quilt look for each block. Mix all cut strips into a basket and set basket on a chair beside your sewing machine.
- Cut 2 - 20 1/2" pink squares
- Cut 2 - 20 1/2" purple squares
- Cut 16 - 2" x 16" black strips for blocks

#1 CENTER STRIP AT LEAST 15 1/2" LONG

Figure 1

Sewing Instructions:
- Begin with a wedge strip for the center, right side up. Place diagonally across 1 - 10 1/2" foundation square. See **Figure 1**. Let the ends of the strip go beyond the corners of the square. Pin in place. Choose your next strip and place it with right sides together on the pinned center strip. Matching raw edges together, sew 1/4" seam allowance from one end to the other end through the two strips and the foundation block (three layers).
- Flip the sewn strip over to its right side, finger press along sewn seam.
- Continue adding strips and sewing to foundation block until one side of the square is completely covered.
- Now sew the strips on the other side of the center wedge and repeat the directions until the foundation square is covered.

- Trim off excess strip lengths to square up block to 10 1/2".
- Do not repeat the same sequence for every block. Offset the center wedge strip so the other blocks will look different.
- Sew 4 - 10 1/2" blocks together for 1 – 20 1/2" block. Repeat for 5 blocks.
- The 4 plain squares have a 2" black strip sewn into a diamond shape.
- Mark the centers of the 4 plain blocks. See **Figure 2**.
- With right sides together, line up a 2" black strip on the center marks and sew to the block. Flip each strip over and press. See **Figure 3**.
- Sew strips and wedges over raw edge of black strips to fill in each corner of square. (The pink square becomes your foundation fabric) Trim off excess to square up block to 20 1/2".

Setting Blocks Together:
- Refer to **Figure 4** for block placement for sewing rows.
- Cut 2" x 60 1/2" black strips for side borders. Attach to quilt.
- Cut 2" x 63 1/2" black strips for top and bottom border. Attach to quilt.
- Quilt in a grid and bind.

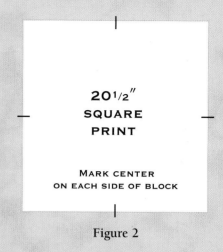

20 1/2"
SQUARE
PRINT

MARK CENTER
ON EACH SIDE OF BLOCK

Figure 2

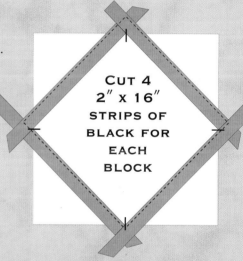

CUT 4
2" x 16"
STRIPS OF
BLACK FOR
EACH
BLOCK

Figure 3

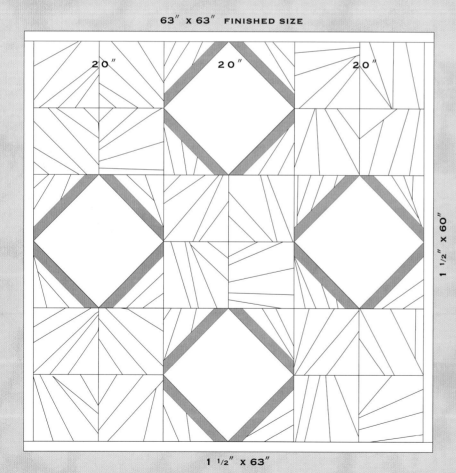

63" x 63" FINISHED SIZE

20" 20" 20"

1 1/2" x 60"

1 1/2" x 63"

Figure 4

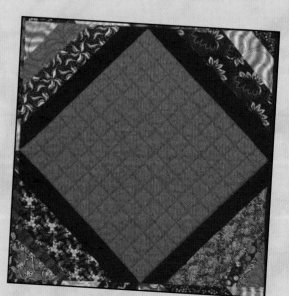

James Deloss Secor and Cynthia Stayner Kennedy Secor
Courtesy Shiloh Museum of Ozark History / Doris Leak Collection (S-84-50-40)

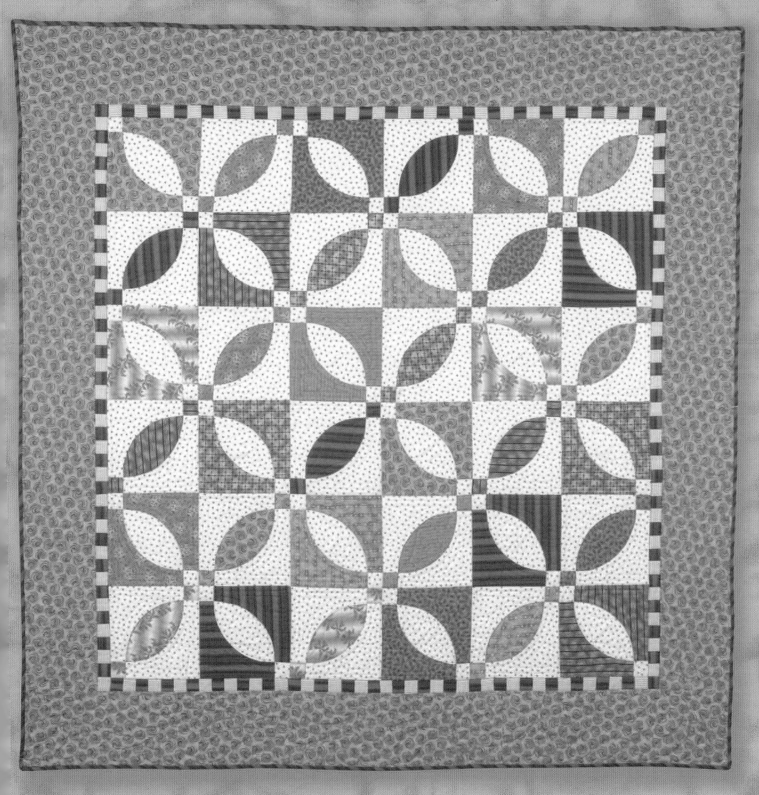

Quilt pieced and set by Pam Mayfield
Quilted by Lori Kukuk

Tennessee Waltz

QUILT SIZE: 56" x 56"

YARDAGE

Each 14" block is made of 4 – 7" blocks with 2 blue and 2 white backgrounds. I used dark to medium shades of blue and chose one white color for all 9 blocks. The checkerboard border nicely separates the blocks from the outside borders.

Blocks - 9 blocks measure 14" finished
• 10-12 fat 1/4's of different shades of medium and dark blues
• 1 3/4 yards of cream or white print
Checkerboard Border – 1" finished squares
• 1/4 yard of dark blue print
• 1/4 yard of light blue print
Borders – 6" finished
• 1 1/2 yards of medium or dark blue

DIRECTIONS

Cutting Instructions:
• Cut 36 blue and 36 white 'A' on straight grain of fabric.
• Cut 18 blue and 18 white 'B'
• Cut 36 blue and 36 white 'D' on straight grain of fabric.
• Cut 43 dark blue and 43 light blue 1 1/2" squares for checkerboard border

Sewing Instructions: Blocks
1/4" seam allowance is shown on templates.
• Piece 18 blue and 18 white 7 1/2" squares for 9 blocks. See **Figure 1**.
• To set the wedges 'B', follow **Figures 2 and 2A**, pinning wedge 'B' curve to wedge, 'D1' curve, right sides together. Sew 1/4" seam, easing in curved edge of 'B' wedge. Do not spare the pins- the more you pin, the easier the bias curve will fit the 'D1' curve.
• Sew 'A' squares on ends of wedge 'D2' see **Figure 3**.
• Set wedge 'B' to the 'D2' piece. See **Figure 4**.
• Set 2 blue and 2 white squares as seen in **Figure 1** to create 1 block. Create 9 blocks.
• Set 3 rows of 3 blocks. Follow **Figure 5** and you will achieve a beautiful chained effect in your quilt.
• Sew 1 1/2" checkerboard squares together alternating dark and light blue. Top and bottom rows have 42 squares and the 2 side rows have 44 squares. Sew top and bottom borders to body of quilt, then sew side borders.

Borders:
• Cut on the cross grain.
• Cut top and bottom borders 6 1/2" x 44 1/2", sew to quilt. See **Figure 6**.
• Cut side borders 6 1/2" x 56 1/2", sew to quilt.

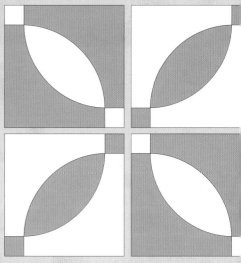

Figure 1

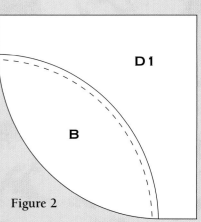

Figure 2

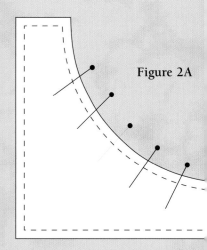

Figure 2A

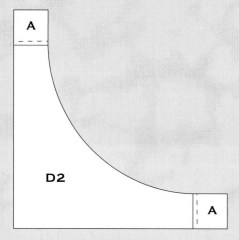

Figure 3

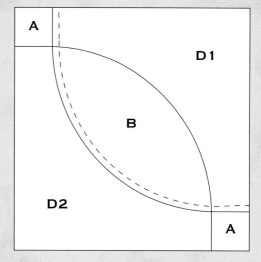

Figure 4

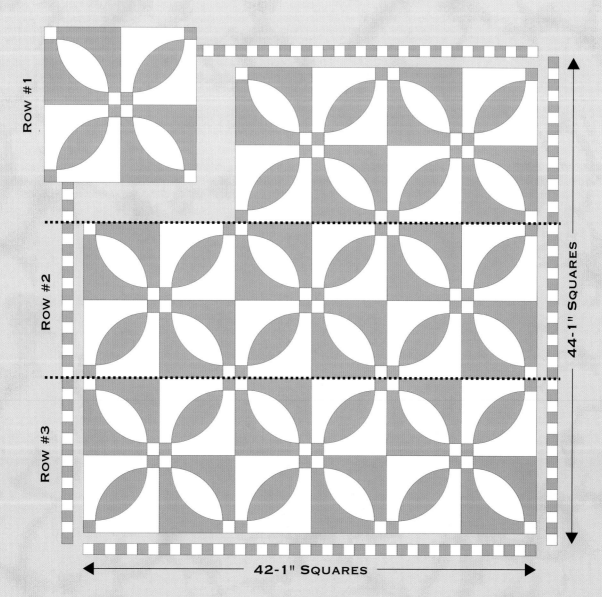

Figure 5

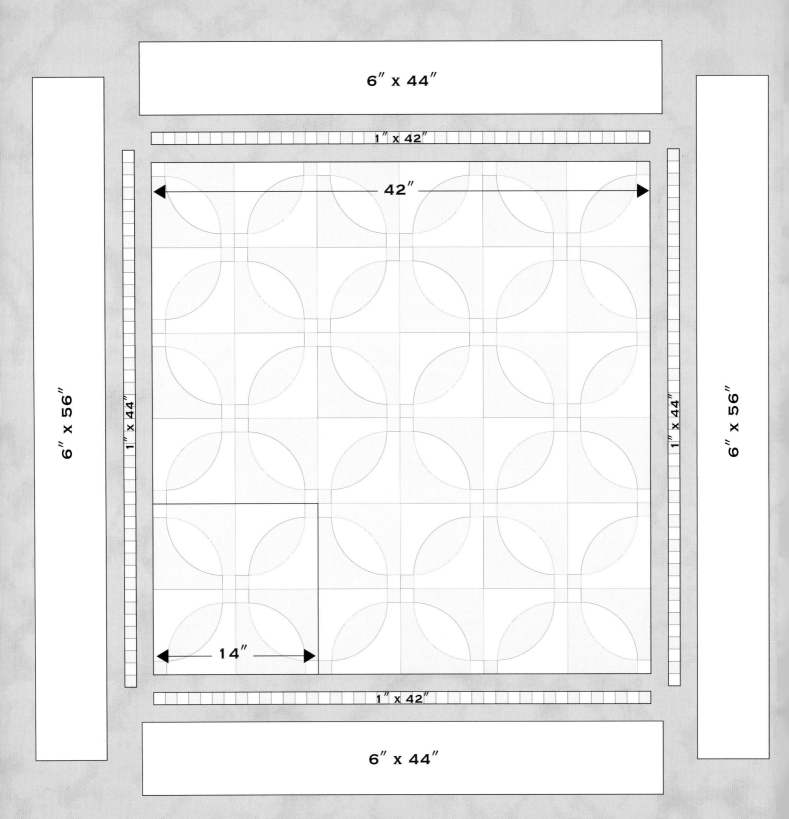

6″ x 44″

1″ x 42″

42″

14″

6″ x 56″

6″ x 56″

1″ x 44″

1″ x 44″

1″ x 42″

6″ x 44″

Figure 6

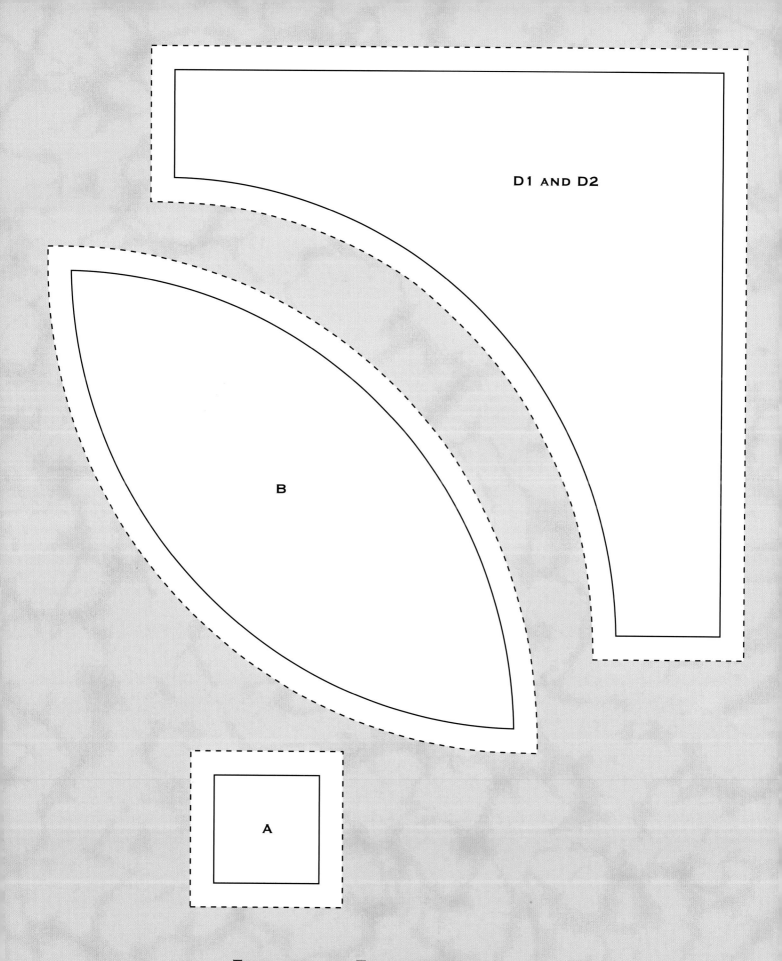

D1 AND D2

B

A

TEMPLATES FOR TENNESSEE WALTZ

21

"Extension Homemakers Club - 50 years of progress" - 1931
Courtesy Shiloh Museum of Ozark History / University of Arkansas: Department of Agriculture Collection (S-85-173-1)

Appliquéd blocks by Jean Stanclift
Quilted by Lori Kukuk

"HOMEMAKERS CLUB" BASKET

QUILT SIZE: 67" x 67"

YARDAGE

- 2 yards yellow for block backgrounds and lattice setting squares
- 1 1/4 yards stripe for baskets and handles
- 3/4 yard light blue for lattice strips
- 2 5/8 yards of dark blue for setting triangles and corners
- 1/4 yard each of shaded or batik in medium blue, dark blue, pink, gold, orange, red, light purple, dark purple, yellow/green, green and dark green for flowers and leaves.
- 1 yard of orange for binding
- 3 1/2 yards light blue print for backing

DIRECTIONS

Cutting Instructions: All Blocks
Add 1/4" seam allowance to all appliqué patterns.
- Cut 13 - 14 1/2" squares for background blocks
- Cut 13 baskets and 13 handles
- Cut 40 leaves 'Z' from various shades of green
- Prepare appliqués for machine or hand sewing

Sewing Instructions:
- Baskets are sewn on point on the 14 1/2" background block. See picture of quilt.
- Center basket and handle on background block
- Sew basket handle in place
- Place basket over handle and sew in place
- All flowers and leaves are set on top of basket

Cutting Instructions:
Flower #1 - Blocks 2, 6, 8 and 12
Add 1/4" seam allowance to all appliqué patterns.
- Cut 6 pink 'A'
- Cut 6 blue 'A'
- Cut 12 orange 'B'
- Prepare appliqués for machine or hand sewing

Flower #2 - Blocks 4, 5, 9 and 10
Add 1/4" seam allowance to all appliqué patterns.
- Cut 3 green 'A'
- Cut 3 red 'A'
- Cut 3 dark purple 'A'
- Cut 3 pink 'A'
- Cut 3 blue 'B'
- Cut 3 yellow/green 'B'
- Cut 3 light purple 'B'
- Cut 3 orange 'B'
- Prepare appliqués for machine or hand sewing

Flower #1

Flower #2

Flower #3 - Blocks 1, 3, 11 and 13
Add 1/4" seam allowance to all appliqué patterns.
• Cut 12 gold 'A'
• Cut 12 blue 'B'
• Prepare appliqués for machine or hand sewing

Flower #4 - Block 7
Add 1/4" seam allowance to all appliqué patterns.
• Cut 1 medium blue 'A' (same as pattern piece 'B'
  of Flower #3)
• Cut 2 dark blue 'B'
• Cut 4 medium blue 'C'
• Cut 2 dark blue 'C'
• Prepare appliqués for machine or hand sewing

Sewing Instructions:
• Assemble flower units.
• Referring to the quilt, place flowers and leaves on
  top of the basket for each block.
• Appliqué to basket.

Cutting Instructions: *Lattice block borders*
& Setting blocks
• Cut 36 - 1 1/2" x 14 1/2" light blue border strips
• Cut 24 - 1 1/2" x 1 1/2" orange squares (same
  as background)
• Cut 2 - 24" dark blue squares. Cut on both diagonals
  for 8 setting triangles.
  See **Figure 1**.
• Cut 2 - 12 1/4" dark blue squares. Cut on the
  diagonal for 4 corner triangles.
  See **Figure 2**.

Flower #3

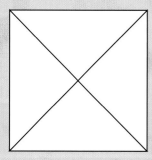

Figure 1

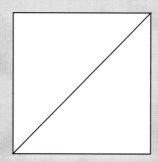

Figure 2

Flower #4

Setting Instructions: *Refer to Figure 3*
Diagonal row #1
• Sew 1 border strip to lower left and 1 to upper right sides of block 1.
• Sew 1 orange square to both ends of 1 strip.
  See **Figure 4**.

SETTING BORDERS

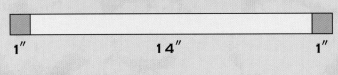

1″   14″   1″

Figure 4

• Sew the strip with the orange squares to the upper left side of block 1.
• Sew 1 corner triangle to the border strip with the orange squares of block 1.
• Sew a dark blue setting triangle to each side of block 1.

Diagonal row 2, 3, 4 and 5
• Sew one blue border strip to the upper left side of each block in the row.
• Sew 1 orange square to one end of the 16 remaining strips.
• Sew one strip (with the orange square at the top) to the bottom left side and one strip to the upper right side of the first block in the row.
• Sew the next block to the upper right strip and then sew a strip with a square to that blocks upper right side. Sew the next block to the strip and so on to complete the rows.
• Sew a setting triangle to the first block and last block of rows 2, 4 and 5.
• Sew a corner triangle to the first and last block of row 3.
• Sew a corner triangle to the lower right side of row 5.
• Sew rows together in order.
• Bind and quilt.

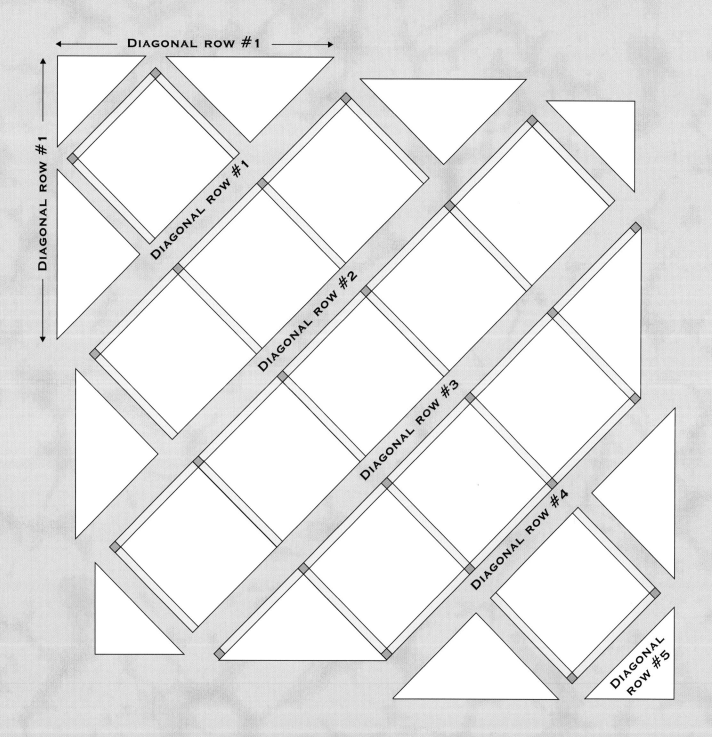

Figure 3

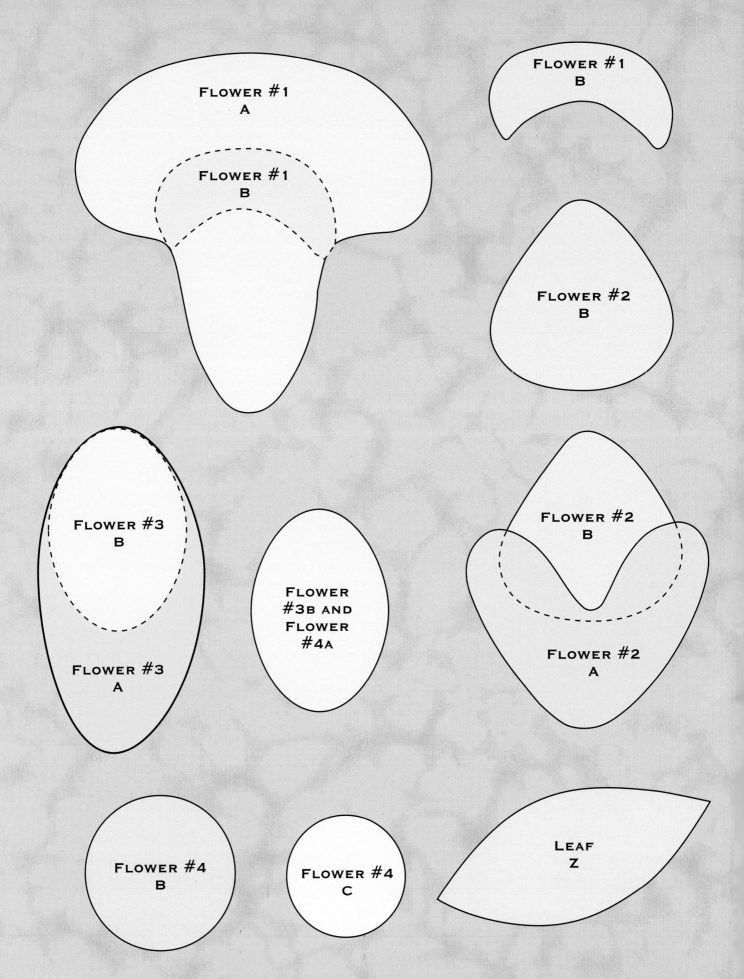

TEMPLATES FOR "HOMEMAKERS CLUB" BASKET

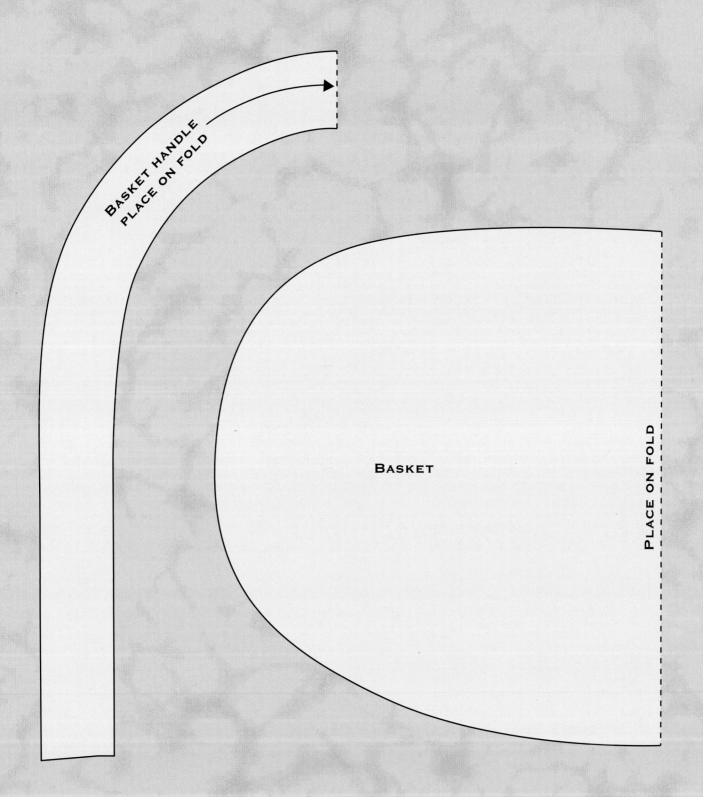

BASKET HANDLE
PLACE ON FOLD

BASKET

PLACE ON FOLD

TEMPLATES FOR "HOMEMAKERS CLUB" BASKET

29

May and Essie Treat
Courtesy Shiloh Museum of Ozark History / Ward Family Collection (S-88-97-30)

Quilt top pieced and set by Pam Mayfield
Quilted by Lori Kukuk

County Fair Cotton Candy

QUILT SIZE: 67" x 81"

YARDAGE

- 12 fat 1/4's of 12 different pink prints
- 12 fat 1/4's of 12 different brown prints
  If you want the same pink and brown prints, buy 1 1/4 yards of pink and 1 1/4 yards brown
- 1 1/4 yards of pink for the finished 1 1/2" narrow border and the 4 -11" finished corner squares
- 3 3/8 yards brown for 11" finished outside borders

DIRECTIONS

Cutting Instructions:
- Cut 24 pink and 24 brown wedges 'A'
- Cut 6 brown and 6 pink center squares 'B'
- Cut 96 pink and 96 brown triangles 'C'

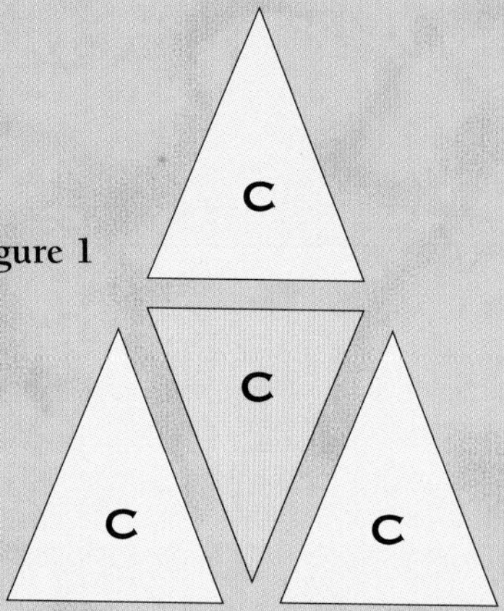

Sewing Instructions:
The blocks alternate pink and brown stars. These figures represent a pink star.
- Refer to **Figures 1 and 2** for color placement and piecing block sections.
- Piece 6 pink star and 6 brown star blocks.

Borders: *Figure 3 shows finished sizes. My directions include the seam allowance.*

Cutting Instructions:
- Cut all borders on the cross grain
- Cut top and bottom narrow pink borders 2" x 42 1/2"
- Cut 2 side narrow pink borders 2" x 59 1/2"
- Cut 4 pink corner squares 11 1/2" x 11 1/2"
- Cut top and bottom brown borders 11 1/2" x 45 1/2"
- Cut 2 side brown borders 11 1/2" x 59 1/2"

Setting Instructions:
- Set 4 rows of 3 blocks each. Alternate pink and brown star blocks.
- Sew top and bottom narrow pink borders to body of quilt.
- Sew side narrow pink borders to quilt.
- Sew side brown borders to quilt.
- Sew an 11 1/2" square to both ends of top and bottom borders.
- Sew top and bottom borders to body of quilt.

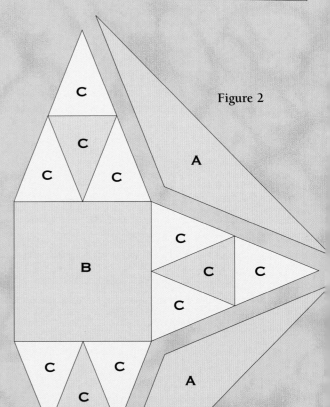

Figure 1

Figure 2

- Quilt, but avoid a fancy design as it will be lost on the printed fabric – chose a 1" diagonal straight line "elbow" pattern for the borders, and a small wreath or flower for the center square and wedges. Bind with a contrasting light brown calico print.

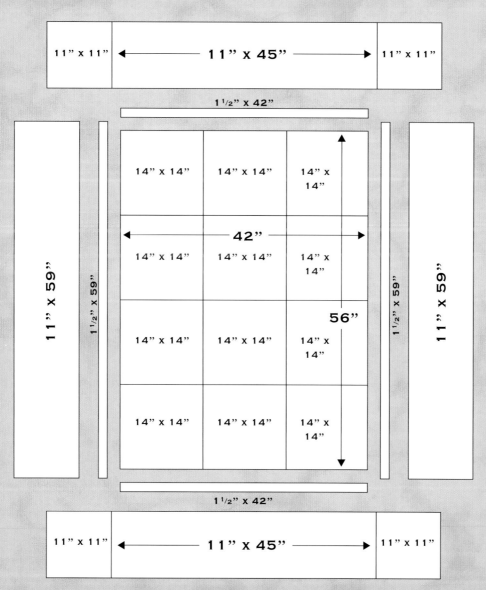

Figure 3

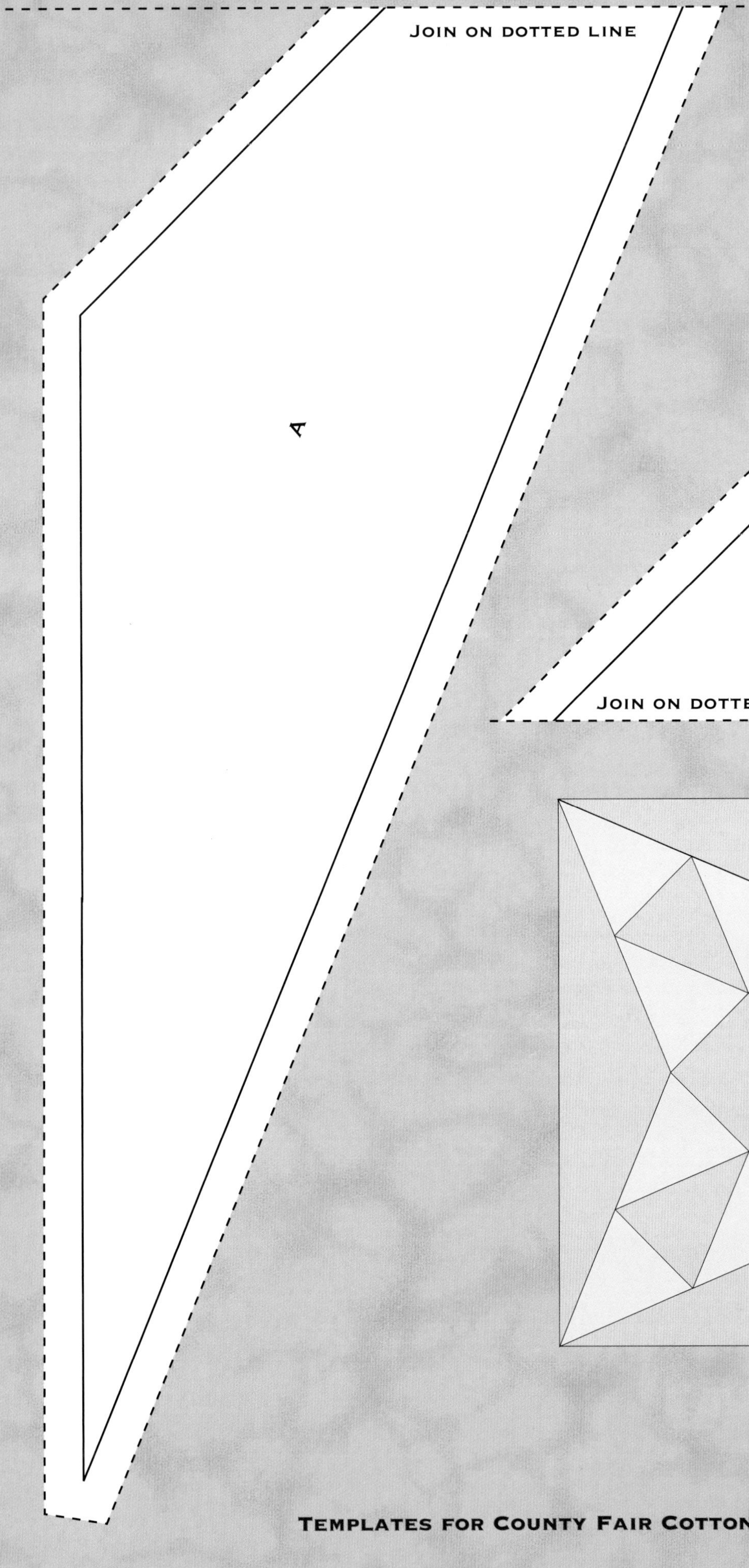

JOIN ON DOTTED LINE

A

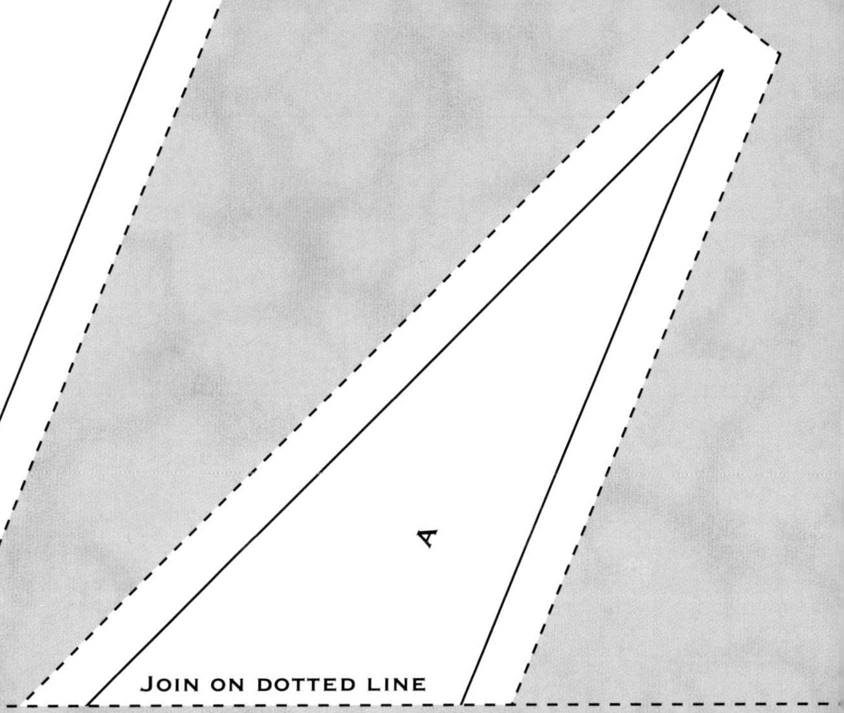

A

JOIN ON DOTTED LINE

TEMPLATES FOR COUNTY FAIR COTTON CANDY

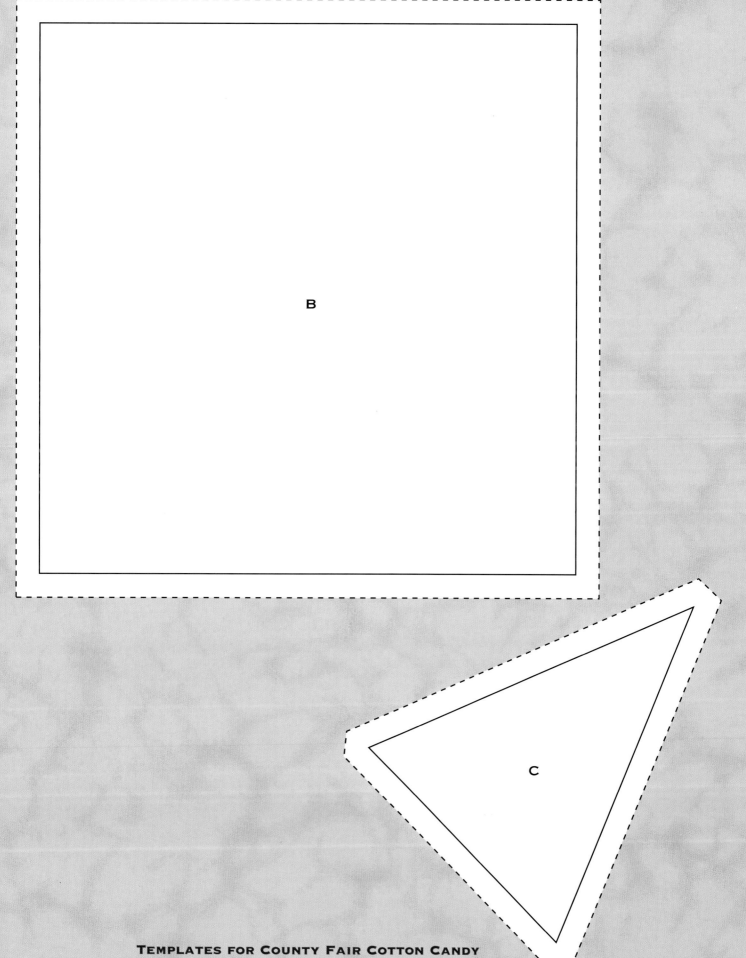

TEMPLATES FOR COUNTY FAIR COTTON CANDY

B

C